Drones

KATIE MARSICO

Children's Press®
An Imprint of Scholastic Inc.

Content Consultant
Matthew Lammi, PhD
Assistant Professor
Department of Science, Technology,
Engineering, and Mathematics Education
North Carolina State University
Raleigh, North Carolina

Library of Congress Cataloging-in-Publication Data
Marsico, Katie, 1980– author.
 Drones / by Katie Marsico.
    pages cm. — (A true book)
 Includes bibliographical references and index.
 ISBN 978-0-531-22480-9 (library binding) — ISBN 978-0-531-22270-6 (pbk.)
 1. Drone aircraft—Juvenile literature. 2. Drone aircraft—History—Juvenile literature. I. Title. II.
Series: True book.
 UG1242.D7M34 2016
 623.74'69—dc23   2015024703

© 2016 Scholastic Inc.
All rights reserved. Published in 2016 by Children's Press, an imprint of Scholastic Inc.
Printed in China 62
SCHOLASTIC, CHILDREN'S PRESS, A TRUE BOOK™, and associated logos are trademarks and/or
registered trademarks of Scholastic Inc.
1 2 3 4 5 6 7 8 9 10 R 25 24 23 22 21 20 19 18 17 16

**Front cover: A DJI Phantom 2 drone flies
over a volcanic eruption
Back cover: A Chilean army drone is
prepared for takeoff during a flight test**

Find the Truth!

Everything you are about to read is true *except* for one of the sentences on this page.

Which one is **TRUE**?

T or F Drones are sometimes used to search for missing persons.

T or F There are no restrictions on flying small drones.

Find the answers in this book.

Contents

THE BIG TRUTH!

From Servers to Shark Spotters

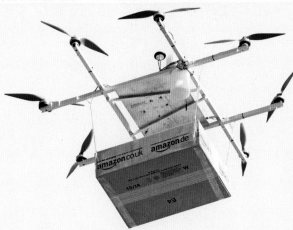

Amazon.com hopes to one day make deliveries with drones.

Hobbyists aren't
allowed to fly drones
over sports stadiums.

NO
DRONES
ALL REMOTE CONTROLLED
AIRCRAFT ARE PROHIBITED

NO

A DJI Phantom 2
drone equipped
with a camera flies
above a 2014 volcanic
eruption in Iceland.

A Unique Flying Force

In fall 2014, hot lava spewed hundreds of feet into the air as a volcano erupted in central Iceland. People around the world were in awe as they viewed close-up video footage of the event. But how did filmmakers get close enough to record this dangerous eruption in such detail? They didn't get close at all. Instead, they attached cameras to drones.

A drone helped people see inside a volcano's crater in Iceland.

What Is a Drone?

A drone, or unmanned **aerial** vehicle (UAV), is a computerized aircraft that does not contain a pilot or passengers. Some drones are able to **navigate** on their own. However, most are piloted from a distance using remote control equipment. This might be as simple as a handheld device with buttons and joysticks. It could also be a complex system that resembles the **cockpit** of a traditional aircraft.

Piloting some drones is a lot like playing a video game.

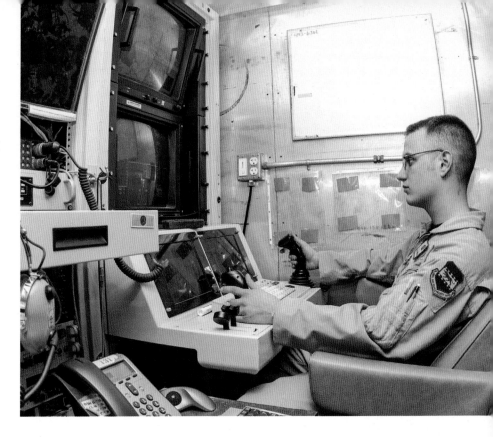

Because they can be very small and no humans are onboard, some drones can reach areas that would otherwise be difficult or dangerous to access. They can fit into tight spaces and glide over difficult terrain. Even if something goes wrong, no passengers or pilots will get hurt. This is why drones were able to safely capture such amazing images of the volcanic eruption in Iceland.

Members of the U.S. and Philippine navies launch a drone during a training exercise.

What Drones Do

Drones can do much more than just record interesting footage. Farmers, scientists, police officers, and countless others have found important uses for these aircraft. They can be used to carry objects from place to place. They can also help locate missing people or hidden artifacts. Militaries often use them for **surveillance** missions and to carry out attacks on distant targets.

Just for Fun

Sometimes people fly drones simply as a hobby. Some enjoy pulling off tricky maneuvers in the air. Others snap photos from high in the sky. Drones are becoming increasingly popular among hobbyists. Simple models can be purchased for less than $100. They are fairly easy to set up and use, and they are available at many stores. This means almost anyone can become a drone pilot.

A drone operator attaches a camera to a drone so he can take photos of a dam.

11

Today's drones are far beyond the simple devices inventors envisioned decades ago.

CHAPTER 2

Past and Present

In 1863, U.S. inventor Charles Perley came up with the idea of a hot-air balloon that could carry explosives. His plan involved attaching a timer to the bombs. When the time was up, the bombs would explode. Unfortunately, the device was unreliable, and Perley's balloons were not widely used. However, other inventors did not give up on the idea of unmanned aircraft.

Drones with helicopter-like propellers can fly up, down, or sideways, and even hover in place.

Wartime Technology

Half a century later, the U.S. Navy began to test unpiloted aircraft during World War I (1914–1918). These aircraft were shaped like airplanes and equipped with bombs. They were launched using catapults. They could then glide toward targets and swoop down to explode. However, the war ended before these aircraft ever played a major role in combat.

The Kettering Bug aerial torpedo was one of the earliest successful drones.

German soldiers prepare a V-1 rocket for launch.

During World War II (1939–1945), unpiloted aircraft took on a new significance in battle. In 1944, Germany unleashed the V-1, an airplane-shaped rocket that could be programmed to fly toward a specific target. Delivering powerful bombs to their targets, V-1 rockets proved to be deadly and effective military tools. Though not technically drones, they helped pave the way for future advances.

With the success of the V-1, other countries began developing their own guided rockets and making improvements to the technology. In the 1950s, U.S. engineers created a device called a cruise missile. Like the V-1, these explosive devices were shaped like airplanes. However, they could be controlled remotely as they flew. Like modern drones, some were even equipped with cameras to make controlling them easier.

Groundbreaking Drones

August 1998
The Aerosonde completes a flight across the Atlantic Ocean.

April 2001
The RQ-4 Global Hawk completes a flight across the Pacific Ocean.

The Next Step

Though guided rockets and missiles were useful for militaries, they had many drawbacks. First, they could be used only one time, as an explosion often destroyed the entire device. Second, they could not fly complex routes. They could be guided, but they had to follow fairly straight paths. To solve these issues, engineers began working to create aircraft more like the drones we know today.

August 2001
The Helios flies at a record altitude of 96,863 feet (29,524 meters).

July 2010
The Zephyr achieves a record nonstop flight time of 14 days.

Cruise missiles were an incredible advance in technology, but they could only be used for attacking enemies.

An Eye in the Sky

In the 1960s, the U.S. military launched the AQM-34 Ryan Firebee. Unlike a cruise missile, this drone could return to base after a mission. The Firebee was able to take photographs and monitor radio communications. It was used to conduct surveillance during the Vietnam War (1954–1975). In the late 1970s, Israeli inventors unveiled Scout, a drone with a built-in television camera that allowed it to transmit live video footage.

Under the Radar

For a surveillance drone to do its job successfully, enemies cannot notice its presence. It must be able to avoid detection by radar systems. One way to do this is to paint the drone with a special coating that keeps radar waves from bouncing off of it. Engineers also protected early drones from radar detection by attaching special blankets to their sides to absorb the waves.

The AQM-34 Ryan Firebee was designed to operate in secret.

Better Than Ever

Advances in technology during the 1980s and 1990s made drones even more effective. Better computers meant improved drone control systems. Better video technology led to drones that could take crystal-clear recordings of their surroundings. New types of sensors enabled drones to collect a variety of additional information about their environment.

Modern drones can take stunning photos and videos from high in the sky.

A world record for altitude was set in 2001 by NASA's Helios drone. It flew at 96,863 feet (29,524 m) above Earth's surface!

Engineers also worked to build new drones capable of flying farther than ever before. In 1998, a drone flew nonstop across the Atlantic Ocean for the first time. The journey took around 27 hours. In 2010, the Zephyr drone was able to stay in the air for more than 336 hours without coming down!

A traffic-monitoring drone flies above the highways of Miami, Florida.

CHAPTER 3

From Massive Tools to Miniature Toys

Today, drones are more than just military technology. There are many different kinds available. Each is suited to different purposes for different people. Police use them to capture footage of traffic accidents and violations such as speeding. Farmers use them to track crop development. Scientists depend on them to monitor everything from weather to natural disasters to endangered wildlife.

Drone data helps clear roads quickly when accidents occur.

Flight Methods

Modern drones come in all shapes and sizes. Some work like helicopters. They are equipped with spinning propellers called **rotor blades**. The rotor blades push air downward, lifting the drone into the sky. Other drones look and function much like airplanes. They have long, narrow bodies with wings on their sides. Engines propel them through the air.

An engineer tests a helicopter drone designed to spray chemicals on crops.

The RQ-4B Global Hawk is one of the most advanced military drones in use today.

An Enormous Drone

The RQ-4B Global Hawk is among the largest drones in use today. It has a wingspan of roughly 131 feet (40 m) and a length of 48 feet (15 m). It is able to cruise at high altitudes and can be operated from as far as 10,000 miles (16,093 kilometers) away. Unlike most drones, the RQ-4B is not entirely controlled remotely. Instead, it relies on an onboard computer and **satellite** signals to help it navigate.

Small and Simple

Not all drones are massive military aircraft. In fact, some are small enough to fit in a pocket. The Wallet Drone—which is primarily used by hobbyists—is one of these "nano drones." It measures roughly 1.6 inches (4 centimeters) in width and length. It is currently being called one of the world's smallest quadcopters. A quadcopter is a drone helicopter equipped with four rotors.

Wallet Drone

The Wallet Drone is not much larger than a quarter.

The Wallet Drone's charger/controller is powered by everyday AA batteries.

The Wallet Drone's small size is a major part of its appeal to hobbyists. It is stored and charged inside a battery-operated remote control about the size of a wallet. This makes it easy for users to transport. After charging for 20 minutes, the Wallet Drone can remain in flight for five to seven minutes. Pilots can use the controller to make it do midair stunts such as rolls and flips.

From Servers to Shark Spotters

It appears highly unlikely that inventors will run out of new uses for drones in the near future. These aircraft are changing everything from restaurant service to archaeology. The innovations described here represent just a handful of the unique jobs that drones perform.

Head's Up!

At the YO! Sushi restaurant chain in London, England, it is especially important for diners to be on the lookout for their meal. Otherwise, they might have a close call with a plate of fast-moving fish! Starting

in 2013, servers at YO! Sushi began flying food to customers on a quadcopter that has been dubbed the iTray. Waitstaff rely on an iPad to control this drone, which is able to zoom at speeds of up to 25 miles per hour (40 kph).

Shark Watching

Just as police officers rely on drones to patrol highways, lifeguards are using drones to watch for sharks. Thanks to shark-spotting drones, people are able to conduct bird's-eye surveillance of what's going on in the water. That way, swimmers aren't endangering themselves by moving through potentially shark-ridden areas. If drones detect sharks behaving aggressively, staff can determine whether to temporarily close nearby beaches.

To Dig or Not to Dig . . .

When archaeologists suspect they may have located a historic site buried beneath the sand, they have to tread carefully. Digging around to determine where artifacts are can be time-consuming. Digging in the wrong spot also carries the risk of disturbing and damaging fragile artifacts. Fortunately, archaeologists can use drones to avoid these difficulties. Drones with special heat-sensing cameras can scan large areas and pinpoint the precise location of archaeological treasures.

CHAPTER 4

The Debate About Drones

Drones can be used in many positive ways. However, their growing popularity also has several downsides. For instance, some people don't believe it is safe for drones to fly through crowded towns and cities. Others are concerned that drones pose a threat to personal privacy. Cities, states, and countries have passed laws restricting drone use. However, these regulations are continually changing.

Hobbyists shouldn't fly drones higher than 400 feet (122 m).

Potential Security Problems

In January 2015, security forces responded to a drone landing on the grounds of the White House in Washington, D.C. Initially, no one knew who was operating the quadcopter or why it was there. Security officials couldn't ignore the possibility that the drone was a threat to the safety of the president and his family.

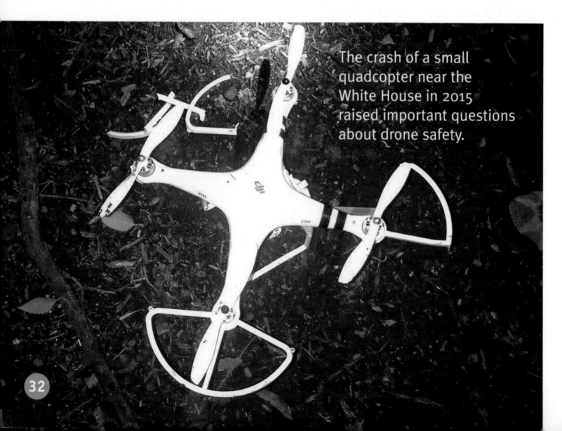

The crash of a small quadcopter near the White House in 2015 raised important questions about drone safety.

Secret Service members performed a thorough search of the White House grounds for additional threats after the drone was discovered.

Ultimately, authorities learned that the incident was purely an accident. The person who had been flying the drone was a hobbyist. He had lost control of the quadcopter outside his apartment. He wasn't even aware of where it had landed. Though the drone's operator didn't face any charges, the episode demonstrated the potential security problems of drone usage.

Some parks and other public areas do not allow drones at all.

Rules and Restrictions

Currently, no license is needed to operate most hobbyist drones in the United States. However, people who want to fly these aircraft for commercial purposes have to pass a written test first. In addition, even hobbyists must be aware of certain airspace restrictions. For example, pilots must keep a specified minimum distance between drones and heavily populated areas. They must also avoid flying the drones too high in the sky.

Some restrictions focus on pilots keeping enough space between their drones and larger aircraft such as airplanes. Operators are also required to keep drones within their eyesight at all times, and they are not allowed to fly at night. Further, hobbyists are generally not supposed to fly drones weighing more than 55 pounds (25 kilograms). Penalties for breaking these guidelines range from fines to criminal charges.

There are strict rules about using drones near buildings.

It is easy to attach a camera to most types of drones.

Accidents and Other Concerns

Despite the rules in place for operating drones, accidents still occur. Beginners who are unfamiliar with the controls run the risk of flying into buildings or even people. Further complications arise when it comes to drones and privacy. Some drones are capable of taking pictures and even capturing video footage. They could easily be used to spy on people in their homes. They could also be used to steal business secrets or other sensitive information.

Currently, the Federal Aviation Administration (FAA) is in charge of setting most regulations on drone usage in the United States. The FAA is the same government agency that sets the rules for other kinds of aircraft. Ideally, rules in the United States and around the world will continue to develop as more people use drones in different ways.

Drone pilots will need to keep a close eye on the latest FAA regulations as new rules are made.

CHAPTER 5

Flying Into the Future

The future of drones is filled with incredible possibilities. For instance, companies such as Amazon.com have plans to use drones to deliver goods to customers. If these plans are successful, people could receive their shipments anywhere. Delivery drones could potentially rely on **GPS** to determine a customer's location at any given moment.

Amazon says its drones will deliver goods in 30 minutes or less.

Facebook has designed an Internet drone that is powered by solar energy.

Providing Internet Access

Meanwhile, social networking sites such as Facebook want to begin using drones to help people access the Internet in areas where it is difficult to get online. Facebook recently revealed its plans to test lightweight drones that can beam down high-speed data via lasers. If effective, these drones would enable residents of remote locations to access the Internet as easily as people in major cities do.

Is It a UFO?

As a growing number of drones fill Earth's skies, it is likely there will be more reports of unidentified flying objects (UFOs). Between 2011 and 2012, there was a 42 percent increase in UFO sightings. Many experts believe this is due to a larger number of drones in the sky. Of course, drones aren't spaceships from another galaxy. However, some manufacturers purposely design them to resemble saucer-shaped UFOs from science-fiction movies.

U.S. Navy employees test a drone.

Drones Everywhere

Inventors are exploring several other potential uses for drones as well. One involves programming these aircraft to serve as tour guides on school campuses and in museums. Militaries around the world also continue to develop drones for combat and surveillance. It is even possible that by 2030 military drones will be soaring overhead at up to six times the speed of sound!

World-Shaping Technology

In the future, drones will be able to travel faster, farther, and higher. Some will be even smaller than today's tiniest drones. Drones will also perform a wider range of functions. Some of these probably seem impossible to imagine at the moment. However, drones have pushed the boundaries of air travel ever since they first appeared in our skies. They are engineering wonders that will undoubtedly continue to shape the world one flight at a time. ★

In the future, drones will likely become more widespread and easier to use than ever before.

True Statistics

Top speed of German V-1 drone: 470 mph (756 kph)

Weight of the bomb the V-1 was equipped to carry: 2,000 lb. (907 kg)

Price at which most hobbyists can purchase a drone: Less than $100

Wingspan of the RQ-4B Global Hawk: Roughly 131 ft. (40 m)

Length of the RQ-4B Global Hawk: Approximately 48 ft. (15 m)

Price of an RQ-4B Global Hawk: $223,000,000

Width of the Wallet Drone: 1.6 in. (4 cm)

Length of the Wallet Drone: 1.6 in. (4 cm)

Did you find the truth?

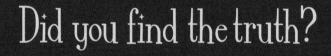

T Drones are sometimes used to search for missing persons.

F There are no restrictions on flying small drones.

NO DRONES
ALL REMOTE CONTROLLED
AIRCRAFT ARE PROHIBITED

NO
FIREW

Resources

Books

Collard, Sneed B. *Technology Forces: Drones and War Machines*. Vero Beach, FL: Rourke Educational Media, 2013.

Henneberg, Susan. *Drones*. Costa Mesa, CA: Saddleback Educational Publishing, 2015.

Nagelhout, Ryan. *Drones*. New York: Gareth Stevens Publishing, 2013.

Wood, Alix. *Drone Operator*. New York: PowerKids Press, 2014.

Visit this Scholastic Web site for more information on drones:
★ www.factsfornow.scholastic.com
Enter the keyword **Drones**

Important Words

aerial (AIR-ee-uhl) — happening in the air

altitude (AL-ti-tood) — the height of something above the ground or above sea level

cockpit (KAHK-pit) — the control area in the front of an aircraft where the pilot and sometimes the crew sit

GPS (GEE PEE ESS) — a system of satellites and devices people use to find out where they are or to get directions to a place; short for "global positioning system"

innovations (in-uh-VAY-shuhnz) — new ideas or inventions

navigate (NAV-uh-gate) — to plan and follow a route

rotor blades (ROH-tur BLAYDZ) — the blades of a helicopter that turn and lift the helicopter into the air

satellite (SAT-uh-lite) — a spacecraft that is sent into orbit around Earth, the moon, or another heavenly body

surveillance (sur-VAY-luhnts) — the process of observing an area to gather information

Index

Page numbers in **bold** indicate illustrations.

About the Author

Katie Marsico graduated from Northwestern University and worked as an editor in reference publishing before she began writing in 2006. Since that time, she has published more than 200 titles for children and young adults. After writing this book, Ms. Marsico is considering purchasing a drone of her own.